Pulleys can be used to pull up a bucket of well water

SIMPLE MACHINES

Pulleys

John Hudson Tiner

A⁺

Smart Apple Media

COPYRIGHT

Published by Smart Apple Media

1980 Lookout Drive, North Mankato, MN 56003

Designed by Rita Marshall

Printed in the United States of America

Photographs by Bonnie Sue, Galyn C. Hammond, The Image Finders (Eric R. Berndt), Derk R. Kuyper, Tom Myers, James P. Rowan, D. Jeanene Tiner

Library of Congress Cataloging-in-Publication Data

Tiner, John Hudson. Pulleys / by John Tiner. p. cm. — (Simple machines)

Includes bibliographical references.

Summary: Discusses how pulleys work and gives examples of pulleys in action.

ISBN 1-58340-136-9

1. Pulleys—Juvenile literature. [1. Pulleys.] I. Title.

TJ1103 .T56 2002   621.8'11—dc21   2001049676

First Edition 9 8 7 6 5 4 3 2 1

Pulleys

CONTENTS

Making Jobs Easier

How does a flag get to the top of a flagpole? Does someone climb the pole? No, the flag is clipped to a rope at the bottom of the pole. The rope goes over a wheel at the top of the pole. Pulling down on the other end of the rope raises the flag. The rope and wheel make a **pulley**. ☐ A pulley can make lifting objects easier. One way a pulley helps is by changing the direction a person must pull. Pulling down to lift a weight feels easier than lifting up. A pulley changes a downward pull into an upward lift. ☐ A farmer may use a pulley to lift hay into a barn

loft. Pulling on a rope lifts the hay into the barn. The farmer has

to pull down hard to lift a bale of hay, but it is easier to move

the hay this way because the farmer's own weight helps.

A pulley raises a flag to the top of a flagpole

Lifting Heavy Loads

Gravity is a force that pulls all things down to earth.

A load, or something to be moved, has weight because of

gravity. To lift a load, a person must pull **Window curtains**

and blinds are

harder than gravity pushes down. The **opened and**

closed by a

force of the person pulling is called the **cord that runs**

through a

effort. ☐ A single, overhead pulley **pulley.**

changes the direction of the force a person applies. But it does

not make the load lighter. To lift a load, a person must pull

down with an effort at least equal to the weight of the load.

Suppose a load weighs more than a person can lift. Adding

more pulleys can improve a person's **lifting power**. Two or

more pulleys can work together to make lifting a load easier.

Using several pulleys can make a load feel lighter

A cable car runs up and down on a giant pulley

With two pulleys, one is placed overhead. The other is attached

to the load. A single rope runs through both of them. The load

is then held by two parts of the rope. This makes the load twice

as easy to lift.

Block and Tackle

A block and tackle is used to lift heavy loads. A block

and tackle has pulleys put together in two groups. One group

of wheels hangs overhead in a holder called a block. The other

wheels are in a lower block. The bottom block rises and lifts

A block and tackle can lift this heavy load of cement

the load hanging from it. ☐ Four pulleys magnify a block

and tackle's lifting power by four. A 100-pound (45 kg) load

can be lifted with a pull of 25 pounds (11 kg). But raising the

load one foot (30.5 cm) takes four **Archimedes (ahr-kih-**

MEE-deez), an ancient

feet (1.2 m) of rope. Even though it **Greek scientist, once**

single-handedly pulled

is easier to raise the load, the rope **a heavy boat onto dry**

land. He used a block

has to be pulled farther. Scientists **and tackle.**

call this "exchanging effort for distance." ☐ **Friction** also

makes it harder to move objects. Two surfaces rubbing to-

gether cause friction. The rope of a block and tackle rubs

against the four wheels. Each wheel causes friction, which robs

some of a person's lifting power.

Pulleys being used to hold a heavy cannon in place

Everyday Pulleys

Pulleys have been used since ancient times. The heavy drawbridge of a castle was hard to close. A weight on the other end of a pulley helped balance the drawbridge. This made the drawbridge easier to pull up and shut. People still use pulleys to raise and lower heavy doors. Many garage doors are opened by a motor that pulls on a belt that runs through a pulley. Some pulleys are very simple. A

An elevator is raised by a motor that pulls on a cable that loops over a pulley.

Pulleys were used to raise and lower drawbridges

crude pulley can be made without a wheel. A man who camps

in a tent may need to keep food away from bears. The man

throws a rope over a high branch. He then ties his food pack

to the rope and pulls it high so bears **Window washers that clean the outside of tall buildings use a block and tackle to move their platforms.**

cannot reach it. The rope and tree branch

make a pulley. Although such a pulley

would not work well in lifting very heavy

loads, it works just fine with light loads. ☐ Some pulleys are

very complex. A **crane** is a machine used to lift heavy loads.

This pulley is used to lift hay into the barn loft

Tall buildings are built with cranes. A crane has a block and tackle that works from the end of a strong metal arm. A steel cable is used instead of a rope, and a powerful motor pulls the cable. No matter how simple or complex, all pulleys help us by changing the direction of a force or magnifying our strength.

A Pulley Experiment

This experiment will prove that a load is easier to lift using a pulley.

What You Need

An empty soft drink can   A rubber band

Three feet (91 cm) of strong string   A cup of water

What You Do

1. Fill the can half full of water.
2. Tie one end of the string to the rubber band. Tie the other end of the string to the soft drink can ring.
3. Set the can on the floor and lift it by pulling up on the rubber band.
4. Notice how far the rubber band stretches.
5. Untie the string from the ring on the can.
6. Run the string through the ring and tie the string to a cabinet drawer.
7. Repeat steps 4 and 5.

What You See

The ring acts as a pulley. How far the rubber band stretches shows the amount of force needed to lift the load. The second time you lifted the can, it was easier because two parts of the string helped lift its weight.

This window washer uses a pulley to climb a building

INFORMATION

Index

Words to Know

crane (KRANE)—a machine for lifting heavy objects; a crane has a block and tackle
   that hangs from a movable arm

effort (EH-fert)—the pushing or pulling force that lifts a load

friction (FRIK-shun)—a force caused by two objects rubbing together; friction tries
   to stop motion

lifting power (LIF-ting pow-er)—the ability to move a load with an effort

pulley (PUH-lee)—a simple machine made of a rope that passes through a wheel

Read More

Ardley, Neil. *The Science Book of Machines*. London: Dorling Kindersley Limited, 1992.

Dunn, Andrew. *Wheels at Work*. New York: Thomson Learning, 1993.

Seller, Mick. *Wheels, Pulleys and Levers*. New York: Shooting Star Press, 1995.

Stephen, R. J. *Cranes*. New York: Franklin Watts, 1986.

Internet Sites

Franklin Institute Online: Simple
Machines
http://www.fi.edu/qa97/spotlight3/
spotlight3.html

How Stuff Works: How a Block and
Tackle Works
http://www.howstuffworks.com/
pulley.htm